I

Benedict XVI

Motu Proprio Data

For the indiction of the Year of Faith

All booklets are published thanks to the generous support of the members of the Catholic Truth Society

CATHOLIC TRUTH SOCIETY
PUBLISHERS TO THE HOLY SEE

APOSTOLIC LETTER
"MOTU PROPRIO DATA"
PORTA FIDEI
OF THE SUPREME PONTIFF
BENEDICT XVI

FOR THE INDICTION OF THE YEAR OF FAITH

1. The "door of faith" (*Acts* 14:27) is always open for us, ushering us into the life of communion with God and offering entry into his Church. It is possible to cross that threshold when the word of God is proclaimed and the heart allows itself to be shaped by transforming grace. To enter through that door is to set out on a journey that lasts a lifetime. It begins with baptism (cf. *Rom* 6:4), through which we can address God as Father, and it ends with the passage through death to eternal life, fruit of the resurrection of the Lord Jesus, whose will it was, by the gift of the Holy Spirit, to draw those who believe in him into his own glory (cf. *Jn* 17:22). To profess faith in the Trinity – Father, Son and Holy Spirit – is to believe in one God who is Love (cf. 1 *Jn* 4:8): the Father, who in the fullness of time sent his Son for our salvation; Jesus Christ, who in the mystery of his death and resurrection redeemed the world; the Holy Spirit, who leads the Church across the centuries as we await the Lord's glorious return.

2. Ever since the start of my ministry as Successor of Peter, I have spoken of the need to rediscover the journey of faith so as to shed ever clearer light on the joy and renewed enthusiasm of the encounter with Christ. During the homily at the Mass marking the inauguration of my pontificate I said: "The Church as a whole and all her Pastors, like Christ, must set out to lead people out of the desert, towards the place of life, towards friendship with the Son of God, towards the One who gives us life, and life in abundance."[1] It often happens that Christians are more concerned for the social, cultural and political consequences of their commitment, continuing to think of the faith as a self-evident presupposition for life in society. In reality, not only can this presupposition no longer be taken for granted, but it is often openly denied.[2] Whereas in the past it was possible to recognize a unitary cultural matrix, broadly accepted in its appeal to the content of the faith and the values inspired by it, today this no longer seems to be the case in large swathes of society, because of a profound crisis of faith that has affected many people.

---

[1] *Homily for the beginning of the Petrine Ministry of the Bishop of Rome* (24 April 2005): AAS 97 (2005), 710.

[2] Cf. Benedict XVI, *Homily at Holy Mass in Lisbon's "Terreiro do Paço"* (11 May 2010): Insegnamenti VI:1 (2010), 673.

3. We cannot accept that salt should become tasteless or the light be kept hidden (cf. *Mt* 5:13-16). The people of today can still experience the need to go to the well, like the Samaritan woman, in order to hear Jesus, who invites us to believe in him and to draw upon the source of living water welling up within him (cf. *Jn* 4:14). We must rediscover a taste for feeding ourselves on the word of God, faithfully handed down by the Church, and on the bread of life, offered as sustenance for his disciples (cf. *Jn* 6:51). Indeed, the teaching of Jesus still resounds in our day with the same power: "Do not labour for the food which perishes, but for the food which endures to eternal life" (*Jn* 6:27). The question posed by his listeners is the same that we ask today: "What must we do, to be doing the works of God?" (*Jn* 6:28). We know Jesus' reply: "This is the work of God, that you believe in him whom he has sent" (*Jn* 6:29). Belief in Jesus Christ, then, is the way to arrive definitively at salvation.

4. In the light of all this, I have decided to announce a Year of Faith. It will begin on 11 October 2012, the fiftieth anniversary of the opening of the Second Vatican Council, and it will end on the Solemnity of Our Lord Jesus Christ, Universal King, on 24 November 2013. The starting date of 11 October 2012 also marks the twentieth anniversary of the publication of the *Catechism of the Catholic Church*, a text promulgated

by my Predecessor, Blessed John Paul II,[3] with a view to illustrating for all the faithful the power and beauty of the faith. This document, an authentic fruit of the Second Vatican Council, was requested by the Extraordinary Synod of Bishops in 1985 as an instrument at the service of catechesis[4] and it was produced in collaboration with all the bishops of the Catholic Church. Moreover, the theme of the General Assembly of the Synod of Bishops that I have convoked for October 2012 is "The New Evangelization for the Transmission of the Christian Faith". This will be a good opportunity to usher the whole Church into a time of particular reflection and rediscovery of the faith. It is not the first time that the Church has been called to celebrate a Year of Faith. My venerable Predecessor the Servant of God Paul VI announced one in 1967, to commemorate the martyrdom of Saints Peter and Paul on the 19th centenary of their supreme act of witness. He thought of it as a solemn moment for the whole Church to make "an authentic and sincere profession of the same faith"; moreover, he wanted this to be confirmed in a way that was "individual and collective, free and conscious, inward and outward, humble and

[3] Cf. John Paul II, Apostolic Constitution *Fidei Depositum* (11 October 1992): *AAS* 86 (1994), 113-118.

[4] Cf. *Final Report of the Second Extraordinary Synod of Bishops* (7 December 1985), II, B, a, 4 in *Enchiridion Vaticanum*, ix, n. 1797.

frank".[5] He thought that in this way the whole Church could reappropriate "exact knowledge of the faith, so as to reinvigorate it, purify it, confirm it, and confess it".[6] The great upheavals of that year made even more evident the need for a celebration of this kind. It concluded with the *Credo of the People of God*,[7] intended to show how much the essential content that for centuries has formed the heritage of all believers needs to be confirmed, understood and explored ever anew, so as to bear consistent witness in historical circumstances very different from those of the past.

5. In some respects, my venerable predecessor saw this Year as a "consequence and a necessity of the postconciliar period",[8] fully conscious of the grave difficulties of the time, especially with regard to the profession of the true faith and its correct interpretation. It seemed to me that timing the launch of the Year of Faith to coincide with the fiftieth anniversary of the opening of the Second Vatican Council would provide a

---

[5] Paul VI, Apostolic Exhortation *Petrum et Paulum Apostolos* on the XIX centenary of the martyrdom of Saints Peter and Paul (22 February 1967): *AAS* 59 (1967), 196.

[6] *Ibid*., 198.

[7] Paul VI, *Credo of the People of God*, cf. Homily at Mass on the XIX centenary of the martyrdom of Saints Peter and Paul at the conclusion of the "Year of Faith" (30 June 1968): *AAS* 60 (1968), 433-445.

[8] Paul VI, *General Audience* (14 June 1967): *Insegnamenti* V (1967), 801.

good opportunity to help people understand that the texts bequeathed by the Council Fathers, in the words of Blessed John Paul II, *"have lost nothing of their value or brilliance*. They need to be read correctly, to be widely known and taken to heart as important and normative texts of the Magisterium, within the Church's Tradition ... I feel more than ever in duty bound to point to the Council as *the great grace bestowed on the Church in the twentieth century*: there we find a sure compass by which to take our bearings in the century now beginning."[9] I would also like to emphasize strongly what I had occasion to say concerning the Council a few months after my election as Successor of Peter: "if we interpret and implement it guided by a right hermeneutic, it can be and can become increasingly powerful for the ever necessary renewal of the Church."[10]

6. The renewal of the Church is also achieved through the witness offered by the lives of believers: by their very existence in the world, Christians are called to radiate the word of truth that the Lord Jesus has left us. The Council itself, in the Dogmatic Constitution *Lumen Gentium*, said this: While "Christ, 'holy, innocent and undefiled' (Heb 7:26) knew nothing of sin (cf. 2 *Cor* 5:21), but came only

---

[9] John Paul II, Apostolic Letter *Novo Millennio Ineunte* (6 January 2001), 57: *AAS* 93 (2001), 308.

[10] *Address to the Roman Curia* (22 December 2005): *AAS* 98 (2006), 52.

to expiate the sins of the people (cf. *Heb* 2:17)... the Church ... clasping sinners to its bosom, at once holy and always in need of purification, follows constantly the path of penance and renewal. The Church, 'like a stranger in a foreign land, presses forward amid the persecutions of the world and the consolations of God', announcing the cross and death of the Lord until he comes (cf. 1 *Cor* 11:26). But by the power of the risen Lord it is given strength to overcome, in patience and in love, its sorrow and its difficulties, both those that are from within and those that are from without, so that it may reveal in the world, faithfully, although with shadows, the mystery of its Lord until, in the end, it shall be manifested in full light."[11]

The Year of Faith, from this perspective, is a summons to an authentic and renewed conversion to the Lord, the one Saviour of the world. In the mystery of his death and resurrection, God has revealed in its fullness the Love that saves and calls us to conversion of life through the forgiveness of sins (cf. *Acts* 5:31). For Saint Paul, this Love ushers us into a new life: "We were buried ... with him by baptism into death, so that as Christ was raised from the dead by the glory of the Father, we too might walk in newness of life" (*Rom* 6:4). Through faith, this new life shapes the whole of human existence according

---

[11] Second Vatican Ecumenical Council, Dogmatic Constitution on the Church *Lumen Gentium*, 8.

to the radical new reality of the resurrection. To the extent that he freely cooperates, man's thoughts and affections, mentality and conduct are slowly purified and transformed, on a journey that is never completely finished in this life. "Faith working through love" (*Gal* 5:6) becomes a new criterion of understanding and action that changes the whole of man's life (cf. *Rom* 12:2; *Col* 3:9-10; *Eph* 4:20-29; 2 *Cor* 5:17).

7. *"Caritas Christi urget nos"* (2 *Cor* 5:14): it is the love of Christ that fills our hearts and impels us to evangelize. Today as in the past, he sends us through the highways of the world to proclaim his Gospel to all the peoples of the earth (cf. *Mt* 28:19). Through his love, Jesus Christ attracts to himself the people of every generation: in every age he convokes the Church, entrusting her with the proclamation of the Gospel by a mandate that is ever new. Today too, there is a need for stronger ecclesial commitment to new evangelization in order to rediscover the joy of believing and the enthusiasm for communicating the faith. In rediscovering his love day by day, the missionary commitment of believers attains force and vigour that can never fade away. Faith grows when it is lived as an experience of love received and when it is communicated as an experience of grace and joy. It makes us fruitful, because it expands our hearts in hope and enables us to bear life-giving witness: indeed, it opens the hearts and minds of

those who listen to respond to the Lord's invitation to adhere to his word and become his disciples. Believers, so Saint Augustine tells us, "strengthen themselves by believing".[12] The saintly Bishop of Hippo had good reason to express himself in this way. As we know, his life was a continual search for the beauty of the faith until such time as his heart would find rest in God.[13] His extensive writings, in which he explains the importance of believing and the truth of the faith, continue even now to form a heritage of incomparable riches, and they still help many people in search of God to find the right path towards the "door of faith".

Only through believing, then, does faith grow and become stronger; there is no other possibility for possessing certitude with regard to one's life apart from self-abandonment, in a continuous crescendo, into the hands of a love that seems to grow constantly because it has its origin in God.

8. On this happy occasion, I wish to invite my brother bishops from all over the world to join the Successor of Peter, during this time of spiritual grace that the Lord offers us, in recalling the precious gift of faith. We want to celebrate this Year in a worthy and fruitful manner. Reflection on the faith will have to be intensified, so as to help all believers in Christ to acquire a more conscious and

---

[12] *De Utilitate Credendi*, I:2.

[13] Cf. Saint Augustine, *Confessions*, I:1.

vigorous adherence to the Gospel, especially at a time of profound change such as humanity is currently experiencing. We will have the opportunity to profess our faith in the Risen Lord in our cathedrals and in the churches of the whole world; in our homes and among our families, so that everyone may feel a strong need to know better and to transmit to future generations the faith of all times. Religious communities as well as parish communities, and all ecclesial bodies old and new, are to find a way, during this Year, to make a public profession of the *Credo*.

9. We want this Year to arouse in every believer the aspiration to *profess* the faith in fullness and with renewed conviction, with confidence and hope. It will also be a good opportunity to intensify the *celebration* of the faith in the liturgy, especially in the Eucharist, which is "the summit towards which the activity of the Church is directed; ... and also the source from which all its power flows."[14] At the same time, we make it our prayer that believers' *witness* of life may grow in credibility. To rediscover the content of the faith that is professed, celebrated, lived and prayed,[15] and to reflect on the act of faith, is a task that every believer must make his own, especially in the course of this Year.

---

[14] Second Vatican Ecumenical Council, Constitution on the Sacred Liturgy *Sacrosanctum Concilium*, 10.

[15] Cf. John Paul II, Apostolic Constitution *Fidei Depositum* (11 October 1992): *AAS* 86 (1994), 116.

Not without reason, Christians in the early centuries were required to learn the creed from memory. It served them as a daily prayer not to forget the commitment they had undertaken in baptism. With words rich in meaning, Saint Augustine speaks of this in a homily on the *redditio symboli*, the handing over of the creed: "the symbol of the holy mystery that you have all received together and that today you have recited one by one, are the words on which the faith of Mother Church is firmly built above the stable foundation that is Christ the Lord. You have received it and recited it, but in your minds and hearts you must keep it ever present, you must repeat it in your beds, recall it in the public squares and not forget it during meals: even when your body is asleep, you must watch over it with your hearts."[16]

10. At this point I would like to sketch a path intended to help us understand more profoundly not only the content of the faith, but also the act by which we choose to entrust ourselves fully to God, in complete freedom. In fact, there exists a profound unity between the act by which we believe and the content to which we give our assent. Saint Paul helps us to enter into this reality when he writes: "Man believes with his heart and so is justified, and he confesses with his lips and so is saved"

---

[16] *Sermo* 215:1.

(*Rom* 10:10). The heart indicates that the first act by which one comes to faith is God's gift and the action of grace which acts and transforms the person deep within.

The example of Lydia is particularly eloquent in this regard. Saint Luke recounts that, while he was at Philippi, Paul went on the Sabbath to proclaim the Gospel to some women; among them was Lydia and "the Lord opened her heart to give heed to what was said by Paul" (*Acts* 16:14). There is an important meaning contained within this expression. Saint Luke teaches that knowing the content to be believed is not sufficient unless the heart, the authentic sacred space within the person, is opened by grace that allows the eyes to see below the surface and to understand that what has been proclaimed is the word of God.

Confessing with the lips indicates in turn that faith implies public testimony and commitment. A Christian may never think of belief as a private act. Faith is choosing to stand with the Lord so as to live with him. This "standing with him" points towards an understanding of the reasons for believing. Faith, precisely because it is a free act, also demands social responsibility for what one believes. The Church on the day of Pentecost demonstrates with utter clarity this public dimension of believing and proclaiming one's faith fearlessly to every person. It is the gift of the Holy Spirit that makes us fit for mission and strengthens our witness, making it frank and courageous.

Profession of faith is an act both personal and communitarian. It is the Church that is the primary subject of faith. In the faith of the Christian community, each individual receives baptism, an effective sign of entry into the people of believers in order to obtain salvation. As we read in the *Catechism of the Catholic Church*: " 'I believe' is the faith of the Church professed personally by each believer, principally during baptism. 'We believe' is the faith of the Church confessed by the bishops assembled in council or more generally by the liturgical assembly of believers. 'I believe' is also the Church, our mother, responding to God by faith as she teaches us to say both 'I believe' and 'we believe'."[17]

Evidently, knowledge of the content of faith is essential for giving one's own *assent*, that is to say for adhering fully with intellect and will to what the Church proposes. Knowledge of faith opens a door into the fullness of the saving mystery revealed by God. The giving of assent implies that, when we believe, we freely accept the whole mystery of faith, because the guarantor of its truth is God who reveals himself and allows us to know his mystery of love.[18]

---

[17] *Catechism of the Catholic Church*, 167.

[18] Cf. First Vatican Ecumenical Council, Dogmatic Constitution on the Catholic Faith *Dei Filius*, chap. III: DS 3008-3009: Second Vatican Ecumenical Council, Dogmatic Constitution on Divine Revelation *Dei Verbum*, 5.

On the other hand, we must not forget that in our cultural context, very many people, while not claiming to have the gift of faith, are nevertheless sincerely searching for the ultimate meaning and definitive truth of their lives and of the world. This search is an authentic "preamble" to the faith, because it guides people onto the path that leads to the mystery of God. Human reason, in fact, bears within itself a demand for "what is perennially valid and lasting".[19] This demand constitutes a permanent summons, indelibly written into the human heart, to set out to find the One whom we would not be seeking had he not already set out to meet us.[20] To this encounter, faith invites us and it opens us in fullness.

11. In order to arrive at a systematic knowledge of the content of the faith, all can find in the *Catechism of the Catholic Church* a precious and indispensable tool. It is one of the most important fruits of the Second Vatican Council. In the Apostolic Constitution *Fidei Depositum*, signed, not by accident, on the thirtieth anniversary of the opening of the Second Vatican Council, Blessed John Paul II wrote: "this catechism will make a very important contribution to that work of renewing the whole life of the Church ... I declare it to be a valid and legitimate

[19] Benedict XVI, *Address at the Collège des Bernardins*, Paris (12 September 2008): *AAS* 100 (2008), 722.
[20] Cf. Saint Augustine, *Confessions*, XIII:1.

instrument for ecclesial communion and a sure norm for teaching the faith."[21]

It is in this sense that that the Year of Faith will have to see a concerted effort to rediscover and study the fundamental content of the faith that receives its systematic and organic synthesis in the *Catechism of the Catholic Church*. Here, in fact, we see the wealth of teaching that the Church has received, safeguarded and proposed in her two thousand years of history. From Sacred Scripture to the Fathers of the Church, from theological masters to the saints across the centuries, the *Catechism* provides a permanent record of the many ways in which the Church has meditated on the faith and made progress in doctrine so as to offer certitude to believers in their lives of faith.

In its very structure, the *Catechism of the Catholic Church* follows the development of the faith right up to the great themes of daily life. On page after page, we find that what is presented here is no theory, but an encounter with a Person who lives within the Church. The profession of faith is followed by an account of sacramental life, in which Christ is present, operative and continues to build his Church. Without the liturgy and the sacraments, the profession of faith would lack efficacy,

---

[21] John Paul II, Apostolic Constitution *Fidei Depositum* (11 October 1992): *AAS* 86 (1994), 115 and 117.

because it would lack the grace which supports Christian witness. By the same criterion, the teaching of the Catechism on the moral life acquires its full meaning if placed in relationship with faith, liturgy and prayer.

12. In this Year, then, the *Catechism of the Catholic Church* will serve as a tool providing real support for the faith, especially for those concerned with the formation of Christians, so crucial in our cultural context. To this end, I have invited the Congregation for the Doctrine of the Faith, by agreement with the competent Dicasteries of the Holy See, to draw up a *Note*, providing the Church and individual believers with some guidelines on how to live this Year of Faith in the most effective and appropriate ways, at the service of belief and evangelization.

To a greater extent than in the past, faith is now being subjected to a series of questions arising from a changed mentality which, especially today, limits the field of rational certainties to that of scientific and technological discoveries. Nevertheless, the Church has never been afraid of demonstrating that there cannot be any conflict between faith and genuine science, because both, albeit via different routes, tend towards the truth.[22]

---

[22] Cf. John Paul II, Encyclical Letter *Fides et Ratio* (14 September 1998), 34, 106: *AAS* 91 (1999), 31-32, 86-87.

13. One thing that will be of decisive importance in this Year is retracing the history of our faith, marked as it is by the unfathomable mystery of the interweaving of holiness and sin. While the former highlights the great contribution that men and women have made to the growth and development of the community through the witness of their lives, the latter must provoke in each person a sincere and continuing work of conversion in order to experience the mercy of the Father which is held out to everyone.

During this time we will need to keep our gaze fixed upon Jesus Christ, the "pioneer and perfecter of our faith" (*Heb* 12:2): in him, all the anguish and all the longing of the human heart finds fulfilment. The joy of love, the answer to the drama of suffering and pain, the power of forgiveness in the face of an offence received and the victory of life over the emptiness of death: all this finds fulfilment in the mystery of his Incarnation, in his becoming man, in his sharing our human weakness so as to transform it by the power of his resurrection. In him who died and rose again for our salvation, the examples of faith that have marked these two thousand years of our salvation history are brought into the fullness of light.

By faith, Mary accepted the Angel's word and believed the message that she was to become the Mother of God in the obedience of her devotion (cf. *Lk* 1:38). Visiting Elizabeth, she raised her hymn of praise to the Most High for the marvels he worked in those who trust him (cf. *Lk* 1:46-55). With joy and trepidation she gave birth to her only son, keeping her virginity intact (cf. *Lk* 2:6-7). Trusting in Joseph, her husband, she took Jesus to Egypt to save him from Herod's persecution (cf. *Mt* 2:13-15). With the same faith, she followed the Lord in his preaching and remained with him all the way to Golgotha (cf. *Jn* 19:25-27). By faith, Mary tasted the fruits of Jesus' resurrection, and treasuring every memory in her heart (cf. *Lk* 2:19, 51), she passed them on to the Twelve assembled with her in the Upper Room to receive the Holy Spirit (cf. *Acts* 1:14; 2:1-4).

By faith, the Apostles left everything to follow their Master (cf. *Mk* 10:28). They believed the words with which he proclaimed the Kingdom of God present and fulfilled in his person (cf. *Lk* 11:20). They lived in communion of life with Jesus who instructed them with his teaching, leaving them a new rule of life, by which they would be recognized as his disciples after his death (cf. *Jn* 13:34-35). By faith, they went out to the whole world, following the command to bring the Gospel to all creation (cf. *Mk* 16:15) and they fearlessly proclaimed to all the joy of the resurrection, of which they were faithful witnesses.

By faith, the disciples formed the first community, gathered around the teaching of the Apostles, in prayer, in celebration of the Eucharist, holding their possessions in common so as to meet the needs of the brethren (cf. *Acts* 2:42-47).

By faith, the martyrs gave their lives, bearing witness to the truth of the Gospel that had transformed them and made them capable of attaining to the greatest gift of love: the forgiveness of their persecutors.

By faith, men and women have consecrated their lives to Christ, leaving all things behind so as to live obedience, poverty and chastity with Gospel simplicity, concrete signs of waiting for the Lord who comes without delay. By faith, countless Christians have promoted action for justice so as to put into practice the word of the Lord, who came to proclaim deliverance from oppression and a year of favour for all (cf. *Lk* 4:18-19).

By faith, across the centuries, men and women of all ages, whose names are written in the Book of Life (cf. *Rev* 7:9, 13:8), have confessed the beauty of following the Lord Jesus wherever they were called to bear witness to the fact that they were Christian: in the family, in the workplace, in public life, in the exercise of the charisms and ministries to which they were called.

By faith, we too live: by the living recognition of the Lord Jesus, present in our lives and in our history.

14. The Year of Faith will also be a good opportunity to intensify the witness of charity. As Saint Paul reminds us: "So faith, hope, love abide, these three; but the greatest of these is love" (1 *Cor* 13:13). With even stronger words – which have always placed Christians under obligation –

Saint James said: "What does it profit, my brethren, if a man says he has faith but has not works? Can his faith save him? If a brother or sister is ill-clad and in lack of daily food, and one of you says to them, 'Go in peace, be warmed and filled', without giving them the things needed for the body, what does it profit? So faith by itself, if it has no works, is dead. But some one will say, 'You have faith and I have works.' Show me your faith apart from your works, and I by my works will show you my faith" (*Jas* 2:14-18).

Faith without charity bears no fruit, while charity without faith would be a sentiment constantly at the mercy of doubt. Faith and charity each require the other, in such a way that each allows the other to set out along its respective path. Indeed, many Christians dedicate their lives with love to those who are lonely, marginalized or excluded, as to those who are the first with a claim on our attention and the most important for us to support, because it is in them that the reflection of Christ's own face is seen. Through faith, we can recognize the face of the risen Lord in those who ask for our love. "As you did it to one of the least of these my brethren, you did it to me" (*Mt* 25:40). These words are a warning that must not be forgotten and a perennial invitation to return the love by which he takes care of us. It is faith that enables us to recognize Christ and it is his love that impels us to assist him whenever he becomes our neighbour along the journey of life. Supported by faith, let us look with hope at our commitment in the world, as we await "new heavens and a new earth in which righteousness dwells" (2 *Pet* 3:13; cf. *Rev* 21:1).

15. Having reached the end of his life, Saint Paul asks his disciple Timothy to "aim at faith" (2 *Tim* 2:22) with the same constancy as when he was a boy (cf. 2 *Tim* 3:15). We hear this invitation directed to each of us, that none of us grow lazy in the faith. It is the lifelong companion that makes it possible to perceive, ever anew, the marvels that God works for us. Intent on gathering the signs of the times in the present of history, faith commits every one of us to become a living sign of the presence of the Risen Lord in the world. What the world is in particular need of today is the credible witness of people enlightened in mind and heart by the word of the Lord, and capable of opening the hearts and minds of many to the desire for God and for true life, life without end.

"That the word of the Lord may speed on and triumph" (2 *Th* 3:1): may this Year of Faith make our relationship with Christ the Lord increasingly firm, since only in him is there the certitude for looking to the future and the guarantee of an authentic and lasting love. The words of Saint Peter shed one final ray of light on faith: "In this you rejoice, though now for a little while you may have to suffer various trials, so that the genuineness of your faith, more precious than gold which though perishable is tested by fire, may redound to praise and glory and honour at the revelation of Jesus Christ. Without having seen him you love him; though you do not now see him you believe in him and rejoice with unutterable and exalted joy. As the outcome of your faith you obtain the salvation of your souls" (1 *Pet* 1:6-9). The life of Christians knows the experience of joy as well as the experience of suffering. How many of the saints have lived in solitude! How many believers, even in our own day, are tested by God's silence when they would rather hear his consoling voice! The trials of life, while helping us to understand the mystery of the Cross and to participate in the sufferings of Christ (cf. *Col* 1:24), are a prelude to the joy and hope to which faith leads: "when I am weak, then I am strong" (2 *Cor* 12:10). We believe with firm certitude that the Lord Jesus has conquered evil and death. With this sure confidence we entrust ourselves to him: he, present in our midst, overcomes the power of the evil one (cf. *Lk* 11:20); and the Church, the visible community of his mercy, abides in him as a sign of definitive reconciliation with the Father.

Let us entrust this time of grace to the Mother of God, proclaimed "blessed because she believed" (*Lk* 1:45).

Given in Rome, at Saint Peter's, on 11 October in the year 2011, the seventh of my Pontificate.

Benedictus PP XVI

BENEDICTUS PP. XVI

CONGREGATION FOR THE DOCTRINE OF THE FAITH

Note with pastoral recommendations for the Year of Faith

Introduction

With the Apostolic Letter of 11 October 2011, *Porta fidei*, Pope Benedict XVI declared a *Year of Faith*. This year will begin on 11 October 2012, on the 50th anniversary of the opening of the Second Ecumenical Vatican Council, and will conclude on 24 November 2013, the Solemnity of our Lord Jesus Christ, Universal King.

This year will be a propitious occasion for the faithful to understand more profoundly that the foundation of Christian faith is "the encounter with an event, a person, which gives life a new horizon and a decisive direction."[1] Founded on the encounter with the Risen Christ, faith can be rediscovered in its wholeness and all its splendor. "In our days too faith is a gift to rediscover, to cultivate and to bear witness to" because the Lord "grants each one of us to live the beauty and joy of being Christians."[2]

---

1. Benedict XVI, Enc. Letter, *Deus caritas est*, 25 December 2005, n. 1.
2. Id., *Homily on the Feast of the Baptism of the Lord*, 10 January 2010.

The beginning of the *Year of Faith* coincides with the anniversaries of two great events which have marked the life of the Church in our days: the fiftieth anniversary of the opening of the Second Vatican Council, called by Blessed Pope John XXIII (11 October 1962), and the twentieth of the promulgation of the *Catechism of the Catholic Church*, given to the Church by Blessed Pope John Paul II (11 October 1992).

The Council, according to Pope John XXIII, wanted "to transmit doctrine, pure and whole, without attenuations or misrepresentations," in such a way that "this sure and immutable teaching, which must be respected faithfully, is elaborated and presented in a way which corresponds to the needs of our time."[3] In this regard, the opening words of the Dogmatic Constitution *Lumen gentium* remain of primary importance: "Christ is the Light of nations. Because this is so, this Sacred Synod gathered together in the Holy Spirit eagerly desires, by proclaiming the Gospel to every creature, (cfr. *Mk* 16:15) to bring the light of Christ to all men, a light brightly visible on the countenance of the Church."[4] Beginning with the light of Christ, which purifies, illuminates and sanctifies in the celebration of the sacred liturgy (cfr. Constitution, *Sacrosanctum Concilium*) and with His

---

3. John XXIII, *Address of the solemn opening of the Ecumenical Vatican Council II*, 11 October 1962.

4. Conc. Ecum. Vat. II, Dogmatic Constitution, *Lumen gentium*, n. 1.

divine word (cfr. Dogmatic Constitution, *Dei Verbum*), the Counil wanted to elaborate on the intimate nature of the Church (cfr. Dogmatic Constitution, *Lumen gentium*) and its relationship with the contemporary world (cfr. Pastoral Constitution, *Gaudium et spes*). Around these four Constitutions, the true pillars of the Council, are arranged the Declarations and Decrees which address some of the major challenges of the day.

After the Council the Church – under the sure guidance of the Magisterium and in continuity with the whole Tradition – set about ensuring the reception and application of the teaching of the Council in all its richness. To assist in the correct reception of the Council, the Popes have frequently convoked the Synod of Bishops,[5] first instituted by the Servant of God, Paul VI, in 1965, providing the Church with clear guidance through the various post-

---

[5] The Ordinary Assemblies of the Synod of Bishops have treated the following topics: *The preservation and strengthening of the Catholic Faith, its integrity, vigor, development, historical and doctrinal coherence* (1967), *The ministerial priesthood and justice in the world* (1971), *Evangelization in the modern world* (1974), *Catechesis in our time* (1977), *The Christian Family* (1980), *Penance and reconciliation in the mission of the Church* (1983), *The vocation and mission of the laity in the Church and in the world* (1987), *The formation of priests in actual circumstances* (1991), *Consecrated life and its mission in the Church and in the world* (1994), *The Bishop: Servant of the Gospel of Jesus Christ for the hope of the world* (2001), *The Eucharist: source and summit of the life and mission of the Church* (2005), *The Word of God in the life and mission of the Church* (2008).

Synodal Apostolic Exhortations. The next General Assembly of the Synod of Bishops, to be held in October 2012, will have as its theme: *The New Evangelization for the Transmission of the Christian Faith*.

From the beginning of his pontificate, Pope Benedict XVI has worked decisively for a correct understanding of the Council, rejecting as erroneous the so-called "hermeneutic of discontinuity and rupture" and promoting what he himself has termed "the 'hermeneutic of reform', of renewal in the continuity of the one subject-Church which the Lord has given to us. She is a subject which increases in time and develops, yet always remaining the same, the one subject of the journeying People of God."[6]

The *Catechism of the Catholic Church*, in this same vein, is both an "authentic fruit of Vatican Council II"[7] and a tool for aiding in its reception. The Extraordinary Synod of Bishops of 1985, convoked on the occasion of the twentieth anniversary of the closing of the Second Vatican Council and to measure its reception, suggested the preparation of a Catechism in order to offer the People of God a compendium of all Catholic doctrine and a sure point of reference for local catechisms. Pope John Paul II accepted this proposal as a desire which "fully

---

6. Benedict XVI, *Address to the Roman Curia*, 22 December 2005.
7. Id., *Porta fidei*, n. 4.

responds to a real need of the universal Church and of the particular Churches."[8] Compiled in collaboration with the entire Episcopate of the Catholic Church, this Catechism "truly expresses what could be called the symphony of the faith."[9]

The *Catechism* includes "the new and the old (cfr. *Mt* 13:52), because the faith is always the same yet the source of ever new light. To respond to this twofold demand, the *Catechism of the Catholic Church* on the one hand repeats the old, traditional order already followed by the Catechism of St Pius V, arranging the material in four parts: the *Creed*, the *Sacred Liturgy*, with pride of place given to the sacraments, the *Christian way of life*, explained beginning with the Ten Commandments, and finally, *Christian prayer*. At the same time, however, the contents are often expressed in a new way in order to respond to the questions of our age."[10] This *Catechism* is "a valid and legitimate instrument for ecclesial communion and a sure norm for teaching the faith."[11] The

---

8. John Paul II, *Address on the closing of the Second Extraordinary Assembly of the Synod of Bishops*, 7 December 1985, n. 6. The same Pope, in the initial phase of this Synod, during the *Angelus* of 24 November 1985, said: "Faith is the principal foundation, it is the cornerstone, the essential criterion of the renewal willed by the Council. From faith come custom, the stile of life and practical direction in every circumstance."

9. Id., Apostolic Constitution, *Fidei depositum*, 11 October 1992, n. 2.

10. *Ibid.*, n. 3.

11. *Ibid.*, n. 4.

content of faith finds " its systematic and organic synthesis in the *Catechism of the Catholic Church*. Here, in fact, we see the wealth of teaching that the Church has received, safeguarded and proposed in her two thousand years of history. From Sacred Scripture to the Fathers of the Church, from theological masters to the saints across the centuries, the *Catechism* provides a permanent record of the many ways in which the Church has meditated on the faith and made progress in doctrine so as to offer certitude to believers in their lives of faith."[12]

The *Year of Faith* is intended to contribute to a renewed conversion to the Lord Jesus and to the rediscovery of faith, so that the members of the Church will be credible and joy-filled witnesses to the Risen Lord in the world of today - capable of leading those many people who are seeking it to the "door of faith." This "door" opens wide man's gaze to Jesus Christ, present among us "always, until the end of the age" (*Mt* 28:20). He shows us how "the art of living" is learned "in an intense relationship with him."[13] "Through his love, Jesus Christ attracts to himself the people of every generation: in every age he convokes the Church, entrusting her with the proclamation of the Gospel by a mandate that is ever

---

12. Benedict XVI, *Porta fidei*, n. 11.

13. Id., *Address to the participants in the meeting organized by the Pontifical Council for the Promotion of the New Evangelization*, 15 October 2011.

new. Today too, there is a need for stronger ecclesial commitment to new evangelization in order to rediscover the joy of believing and the enthusiasm for communicating the faith."[14]

At the invitation of Pope Benedict XVI,[15] the Congregation for the Doctrine of the Faith, in consultation with the competent Dicasteries of the Holy See and with the contribution of the *Committee for the Preparation of the Year of Faith*,[16] has drawn up this *Note*, with some recommendations for living this time of grace, without precluding other initiatives which the Holy Spirit will inspire among Pastors and faithful in various parts of the world.

Recommendations

"I know him in whom I have believed" (2 *Tm* 1:12). These words of St Paul help us to understand that faith is "first of all a personal adherence of man to God. At the

---

14. Id., Apostolic Letter, *Porta fidei*, n. 7.

15. Cfr. *ibid.*, n. 12.

16. This *Committee*, formed by the Congregation for the Doctrine of the Faith, according to the mandate of the Holy Father, Benedict XVI, includes among its members: Cardinals William Levada, Francis Arinze, Angelo Bagnasco, Ivan Dias, Francis E. George, Zenon Grocholewski, Marc Ouellet, Mauro Piacenza, Jean-Pierre Ricard, Stanisław Ryłko and Christoph Schönborn; Archbishops Luis F. Ladaria, and Salvatore Fisichella; Bishops Mario del Valle Moronta Rodríguez, Gerhard Ludwig Müller and Raffaello Martinelli.

same time, and inseparably, it is a free assent to the whole truth that God has revealed."[17] Faith which is a personal trust in the Lord and the faith which we profess in the Creed are inseparable; they focus on each other and they require each other. There exists a profound bond between the lived faith and its contents. The faith of the Witnesses and Confessors is also the faith of the Apostles and Doctors of the Church.

Thus, the following recommendations for the *Year of Faith* desire to aid both the encounter with Christ through authentic witnesses to faith, and the ever-greater understanding of its contents. These proposals are intended as examples to encourage a ready response to the invitation of the Holy Father to live fully this *Year* as a special "time of grace."[18] The joyous rediscovery of faith can also contribute to consolidate the unity and communion among the different bodies that make up the wider family of the Church.

I. On the level of the Universal Church

1. The main ecclesial event at the beginning of the *Year of Faith* will be the XIII General Assembly of the Ordinary Synod of Bishops, convoked by Pope Benedict XVI in October 2012, dedicated to *The New Evangelization for the Transmission of the Christian*

---

[17] *Catechism of the Catholic Church*, n. 150.

[18] Benedict XVI, Apostolic Letter, *Porta fidei*, n. 15.

Faith. During this Synod, on 11 October 2012, there will be a solemn celebration of the beginning of the *Year of Faith*, in remembrance of the fiftieth anniversary of the opening of the Second Vatican Council.

2. In the *Year of Faith* pilgrimages of the faithful to the See of Peter are to be encouraged, to profess faith in God the Father, Son and Holy Spirit, in unity with him who today is called to confirm his brothers and sisters in the faith (cfr. *Lk* 22:32). It is also important to promote pilgrimages to the Holy Land, the place which first saw the presence of Jesus, the Savior, and Mary, his Mother.

3. During this *Year*, it will be helpful to invite the faithful to turn with particular devotion to Mary, model of the Church, who "shines forth to the whole community of the elect as the model of virtues."[19] Therefore, every initiative that helps the faithful to recognize the special role of Mary in the mystery of salvation, love her and follow her as a model of faith and virtue is to be encouraged. To this end it would be proper to organize pilgrimages, celebrations and gatherings at the major Marian shrines.

4. The next World Youth Day, in Rio de Janeiro in July 2013, will offer a special occasion for the young to experience the joy which comes from faith in the Lord

---

19. Conc. Ecum. Vat. II, Dogmatic Constitution, *Lumen gentium*, n. 65.

Jesus and communion with the Holy Father, in the greater family of the Church.

5. It is hoped that many symposia, conferences and large gatherings will be held, even at the international level, to encourage encounters with authentic witness to the faith and to promote understanding of the contents of Catholic doctrine. Noting how, still today, the Word of God continues to grow and spread, it will be important to give witness that "all the anguish and all the longing of the human heart finds fulfilment"[20] in Christ Jesus and that faith "becomes a new criterion of understanding and action that changes the whole of man's life."[21] Some conferences should be particularly dedicated to the rediscovery of the teachings of Vatican Council II.

6. The *Year of Faith* will offer a special opportunity for all believers to deepen their knowledge of the primary documents of the Second Vatican Council and their study of the *Catechism of the Catholic Church*. This is especially true for candidates for priesthood, particularly during the propeduetic year or in their first years of theological studies, for novices in Institutes of Consecrated Life and Societies of Apostolic Life, as well as for those in a period of discernment for joining an Ecclesial Association or Movement.

---

20. Benedict XVI, Apostolic Letter, *Porta fidei*, n. 13.

21. *Ibid*., n. 6.

7. This *Year* will provide an auspicious time for a more attentive reception of the homilies, catechesis, addresses and other speeches and documents of the Holy Father. Pastors, consecrated persons and the lay faithful are invited to renew their efforts in effective and heart-felt adherence to the teaching of the Successor of Peter.

8. During the *Year of Faith*, in cooperation with the Pontifical Council for the Promotion of Christian Unity, various ecumenical initiatives are to be planned, aimed at "the restoration of unity among all Christians" which "is one of the principal concerns of the Second Vatican Council."[22] In particular, there will be a solemn ecumenical celebration in which all of the baptized will reaffirm their faith in Christ.

9. A *Secretariat* to coordinate all of the different initiatives promoted by various Dicasteries of the Holy See, or other events relevant to the Universal Church, will be established within the Pontifical Council for the Promotion of the New Evangelization. This *Secretariat* should be informed timely of the main events and can also suggest appropriate initiatives. The *Secretariat* will open a dedicated website with the goal of making available useful information regarding living out the *Year of Faith* more effectively.

---

[22] Conc. Ecum. Vat. II, Decree, *Unitatis redintigratio*, n. 1.

10. At the conclusion of this *Year*, on the Solemnity of Our Lord Jesus Christ, Universal King, there will be a Eucharist celebrated by the Holy Father, in which a solemn renewal of the profession of faith will take place.

II. On the level of Episcopal Conferences[23]

1. Episcopal Conferences, in light of the specific mission of the Bishops as teachers and "heralds of the faith,"[24] can dedicate a day of study to the topic of faith, its personal witness and its transmission to new generations.

2. The republication in paperback and economical editions of the Documents of Vatican Council II, the *Catechism of the Catholic Church* and its *Compendium* is to be promoted, as is the wider distribution of these texts through electronic means and modern technologies.

3. A renewed effort to translate the documents of Vatican Council II and the *Catechism of the Catholic Church* into languages which lack a translation is desirable. Initiatives of charitable support to enable translations into the local languages of mission countries, where the local Churches

---

23. The following recommendations made for Episcopal Conferences are also offered, in an analogous way, to the Synods of Bishops of Patriarchal and Major Archepiscopal Churches, as well as to the Assemblies of Hierarchs of the other Eastern Catholic Churches sui iuris.

24. Conc. Ecum. Vat. II, Dogmatic Constitution, *Lumen gentium*, n. 25.

cannot afford the expense, are to be encouraged. This should be done under the guidance of the Congregation for the Evangelization of Peoples.

4. Pastors should work to promote television and radio transmissions, films and publications focusing on the faith, its principles and content, as well as on the ecclesial significance of the Second Vatican Council. This should be done using the new styles of communication, especially on the popular level, making these things available to a wider public.

5. The Saints and the Blessed are the authentic witnesses of the faith.[25] It is, therefore, opportune that Episcopal Conferences work toward the dissemination of a knowledge of the local Saints of their territory, also by modern means of social communication.

6. The contemporary world is sensitive to the relationship between faith and art. It is, therefore, recommended that Episcopal Conferences maximize the catechetical potential – possibly with ecumenical cooperation – of the artistic patrimony of the region entrusted to their pastoral care.

7. Educators in centers of theological studies, seminaries and Catholic universities should be encouraged in their teaching to demonstrate the relevance within their various

---

25. Benedict XVI, Apostolic Letter, *Porta fidei*, n. 13.

disciplines of the contents of the *Catechism of the Catholic Church* and of the implications derived from them.

8. It would be useful to arrange for the preparation of pamphlets and leaflets of an apologetic nature (cfr. 1 *Pt* 3:15), which should be done with the help of theologians and authors. Every member of the faithful would then be enabled to respond better to the questions which arise in difficult contexts – whether to do with sects, or the problems related to secularism and relativism, or to questions "arising from a changed mentality which, especially today, limits the field of rational certainties to that of scientific and technological discoveries,"[26] or to other specific issues.

9. It is hoped that local catechisms and various catechetical supplements in use in the particular Churches would be examined to ensure their complete conformity with the *Catechism of the Catholic Church*.[27] Should a catechism or supplement be found to be not totally in accord with the *Catechism*, or should some lacunae be discovered, new ones should be developed, following the example of those Conferences which have already done so.

10. The *Year of Faith* will also be an appropriate time to examine, in collaboration with the Congregation for Catholic Education, the *Ratio* of formation for future

26. *Ibid.*, n. 12.

27. John Paul II, Apostolic Constitution, *Fidei depositum*, n. 4.

priests, ensuring that the contents of the *Catechism for the Catholic Church* are present in their theological studies.

III. At the Diocesan level

1. It is hoped that each particular Church would have a celebration of the opening of the *Year of Faith* and a solemn conclusion to it, in which to "profess our faith in the Risen Lord in our cathedrals and in the churches of the whole world."[28]

2. It would be desirable that each Diocese in the world organize a study day on the *Catechism of the Catholic Church*, particularly for its priests, consecrated persons and catechists. On this occasion, for example, the Eastern Catholic Eparchies could hold a meeting with their priests to give witness to their specific experience and liturgical tradition in the one faith in Christ. Also, in this way, young particular Churches in mission territories would be able to give renewed witness to that joy of faith which is so often particular to them.

3. Each Bishop could devote a pastoral letter of his own to the topic of faith, keeping in mind the specific pastoral circumstances of the portion of the faithful entrusted to him, reminding them of the importance of the Second Vatican Council and of the *Catechism of the Catholic Church*.

---

[28] Benedict XVI, Apostolic Letter, *Porta fidei*, n. 8.

4. It is hoped that in each Diocese, under the leadership of the Bishop, catechetical events will be organized, especially for the youth and those searching for a sense of life, helping them to discover the beauty of ecclesial faith, promoting encounters with meaningful witnesses to the faith.

5. It would be appropriate for each particular Church to review the reception of Vatican Council II and the *Catechism of the Catholic Church* in its own life and mission, particularly in the realm of catechesis. This would provide the opportunity for a renewal of commitment on the part of the catechetical offices of the Dioceses which - supported by the Commissions for Catechesis of the Episcopal Conferences – have the duty to care for the theological formation of catechists.

6. The continuing education of the clergy can be focused during this *Year of Faith* on the documents of Vatican Council II and on the *Catechism of the Catholic Church*, treating such themes as "the proclamation of the Risen Christ", "the Church - sacrament of salvation", "the mission of evangelization in the world today", "faith and disbelief", "faith, ecumenism and inter-religious dialogue", "faith and eternal life", "the hermeneutic of reform in continuity" and "the *Catechism* in ordinary pastoral care."

7. Bishops are invited to organize penitential celebrations, particularly during Lent, in which all can ask for God's forgiveness, especially for sins against faith. This *Year* also provides an appropriate occasion in which all can approach the Sacrament of Penance with greater faith and more frequently.

8. It is hoped that there will be a renewed creative dialogue between faith and reason in the academic and artistic communities, through symposia, meetings and days of study, especially at Catholic universities, in order to demonstrate that "there cannot be any conflict between faith and genuine science, because both, albeit via different routes, tend towards the truth."[29]

9. It is also important to promote encounters with those persons who, "while not claiming to have the gift of faith, are nevertheless sincerely searching for the ultimate meaning and definitive truth of their lives and of the world,"[30] taking as an example the dialogues of the *Courtyard of the Gentiles*, sponsored by the Pontifical Council for Culture.

10. The *Year of Faith* can be an opportunity to pay greater attention to Catholic schools, which are a perfect place to offer to students a living witness to the Lord and

---

29. *Ibid.*, n. 12.
30. *Ibid.*, n. 10.

to nurture their faith. This can be done by making use of good catechetical tools, like the *Compendium of the Catechism of the Catholic Church* and *Youcat*.

IV. At the level of the parish/community/association/movement

1. In preparation for the *Year of Faith*, all of the faithful are invited to read closely and meditate upon Pope Benedict XVI's Apostolic Letter, *Porta fidei*.

2. The *Year of Faith* "will also be a good opportunity to intensify the *celebration* of the faith in the liturgy, especially in the Eucharist."[31] In the Eucharist, mystery of faith and source of the new evangelization, the faith of the Church is proclaimed, celebrated and strengthened. All of the faithful are invited to participate in the Eucharist actively, fruitfully and with awareness, in order to be authentic witnesses of the Lord.

3. Priests should devote greater attention to the study of the documents of Vatican Council II and the *Catechism of the Catholic Church*, drawing from them resources for the pastoral care of their parishes – catechesis, preaching, Sacramental preparation. They should also offer cycles of homilies on the faith or on certain specific aspects such as,

---

[31] *Ibid.*, n. 9.

for example, "the encounter with Christ", "the fundamental contents of the Creed", and "faith and the Church."[32]

4. Catechists should hold more firmly to the doctrinal richness of the *Catechism of the Catholic Church* and, under the direction of their pastors, offer guidance in reading this precious document to groups of faithful, working toward a deeper common understanding thereof, with the goal of creating small communities of faith, and of giving witness to the Lord Jesus.

5. It is hoped that there will be a renewed commitment in parishes to the distribution of the *Catechism of the Catholic Church*, and of other resources appropriate for families, which are true domestic churches and the primary setting for the transmission of the faith. This might be done, for example, during the blessing of homes, the Baptism of adults, Confirmations and Marriages. This can contribute to the deepening of Catholic teaching "in our homes and among our families, so that everyone may feel a strong need to know better and to transmit to future generations the faith of all times."[33]

---

32. Cfr., Benedict XVI, Apostolic Exhortation, *Verbum Domini*, 30 September 2010, nn. 59-60, and 74.
33. ID., Apostolic Letter, *Porta fidei*, n. 8.

6. The promotion of *missions* and other popular programs in parishes and in the workplace can help the faithful to rediscover the gift of Baptismal faith and the task of giving witness, knowing that the Christian vocation "by its very nature is also a vocation to the apostolate."[34]

7. During this time, members of Institutes of Consecrated Life and of Societies of Apostolic Life are asked to work towards the new evangelization with a renewed union to the Lord Jesus, each according to their proper charism, in fidelity to the Holy Father and to sound doctrine.

8. Contemplative communities, during the *Year of Faith*, should pray specifically for the renewal of the faith among the People of God and for a new impulse for its transmission to the young.

9. Associations and Ecclesial Movements are invited to promote specific initiatives which, through the contribution of their proper charism and in collaboration with their local Pastors, will contribute to the wider experience of the *Year of Faith*. The new Communities and Ecclesial Movements, in a creative and generous way, will be able to find the most appropriate ways in which to offer their witness to the faith in service to the Church.

10. All of the faithful, called to renew the gift of faith, should try to communicate their own experience of faith

[34] Conc. Ecum. Vat. II, Decree, *Apostolicam actuositatem*, n. 2.

and charity[35] to their brothers and sisters of other religions, with those who do not believe, and with those who are just indifferent. In this way, it is hoped that the entire Christian people will begin a kind of mission toward those with whom they live and work, knowing that they "have welcomed the news of salvation which is meant for every man."[36]

Conclusion

Faith "is the lifelong companion that makes it possible to perceive, ever anew, the marvels that God works for us. Intent on gathering the signs of the times in the present of history, faith commits every one of us to become a living sign of the presence of the Risen Lord in the world."[37] Faith is both a personal and a communal act: it is a gift from God that is lived in the communion of the Church and must be communicated to the world. Every initiative for the *Year of Faith* should be designed to aid in the joyous rediscovery of the faith and its renewed transmission. The recommendations provided here have the goal of inviting all of the members of the Church to work so that this *Year* may be a special time in which we, as Christians, may share that which is most dear to us: Christ Jesus, the Redeemer of mankind, Universal King, "leader and perfecter of faith" (*Heb* 12:2).

---

35. Cfr. Benedict XVI, Apostolic Letter, *Porta fidei*, n. 14.
36. Conc. Ecum. Vat. II, Pastoral Constitution, *Gaudium et spes*, n. 1.
37. Benedict XVI, Apostolic Letter, *Porta fidei*, n. 15.

Given in Rome, at the Congregation for the Doctrine of the Faith, on 6 January 2012, the Solemnity of the Epiphany of the Lord.

William Cardinal Levada
Prefect

Luis F. Ladaria, S.J.
Secretary